THE AUTHOR'S GUIDE TO
CONFLICT
RESOLUTION

A revolutionary approach
to effective collaboration

JANE GUNN

The Authority Guide to Conflict Resolution

A revolutionary approach to effective collaboration

© Jane Gunn

ISBN 978-1-912300-06-8

eISBN 978-1-912300-07-5

Published in 2017 by Authority Guides

authorityguides.co.uk

The right of Jane Gunn to be identified as the author
of this work has been asserted by her in accordance with the
Copyright, Designs and Patents Act 1988.

A CIP record of this book is available from the British Library.

All rights reserved. No part of this book may be reproduced, stored
in a retrieval system, or transmitted in any form or by any means,
electronic, mechanical, photocopying, recording or otherwise,
without the prior written permission of the publisher.

No responsibility for loss occasioned to any person acting or
refraining from action as a result of any material in this publication
can be accepted by the author or publisher.

Note on references: if I have inadvertently used any words or materials
without acknowledging the originator, I apologise and would be happy to
include a reference in the next edition.

Cartoons created by Simon Ellinas

© Jane Gunn

Printed in the United Kingdom.

Acknowledgements

I'd like to dedicate this book to *all* my family, friends, colleagues and clients with whom I have collaborated over the years. It has been an honour to work/live/play with you and I have learnt such a lot from our time together. Without you and the thoughts, ideas and experiences we have shared, I would not be where I am today.

To all of the team at SRA and in particular Sue Richardson, Kelly Mundt and Christopher Cudmore, thank you for your enthusiasm and encouragement.

To Kriss Akabusi and Steve Head, my mastermind buddies, thank you for all that we have shared over the years, our failures as well as our successes and for continually challenging me to be and do the best that I can.

To my husband Rob and daughters Victoria and Rebecca, a huge thank you for cheering me on for so many years and enabling me to do what I love.

How soon 'not now' becomes 'never'.

Martin Luther

Contents

In quarrelling, the truth is always lost.

Publilius Syrus

Introduction – collaborate or die?

In today's economy some businesses will die, some will survive and some will see the opportunities it presents and thrive.

One of the essential skills that will define the survivors is the ability to collaborate.

As a business leader or entrepreneur you need to create strong collaborative relationships with all of your organisational stake-holders – with everyone who enables your organisation to grow and develop. You must also actively seek out new opportunities to collaborate to take your business to the next level.

But do you have the right knowledge and skills to create strong collaborative relationships? Do you know how to avoid the pitfalls and conflicts and make sure that you are adding value and not risking loss? Imagine the benefits if you could capture the energy and dynamism that different personalities and approaches bring, as opposed to clashes and conflicts that often cost time, productivity and money.

You want to achieve your potential – to be successful and happy – both at work and at home *but* you live and work with others who don't always agree or see things the same way. Your ability to deal with the challenges and crises in the relationships with your colleagues, friends and family comes down to how effectively you can manage conflict.

There is unbelievable power in the skills and tools that help you to build confidence in dealing with people when you don't see eye to eye. People do not connect to those who believe they are better than or more right than they are; rather they connect to those who are able to listen to and acknowledge the needs, interests and concerns of others, alongside their own.

I believe strongly that conflict is *the key* to effective collaboration. We cannot work together unless we both acknowledge and actively manage the issues that arise every day. And yet, our instinctive approach is often to avoid such issues or to behave in an aggressive or adversarial way that damages or destroys the very relationships on which we depend to live and work happily and effectively.

How to use this book

This *Authority Guide* will teach you the skills I have developed during 30 years working both as a lawyer and mediator helping people and businesses transform relationships. Based on subjects that I've been asked about consistently in my workshops and training, we'll be looking at, and answering, these key questions:

- What is conflict?
- Why is conflict magic?
- What are some common issues that cause conflict?
- What is the cost of unresolved conflict?
- Who are my stakeholders?

- Why don't I say what's on my mind?

- Why do you and I see things differently?

- Why don't I behave/act as I would like to?

- Why does conflict escalate so quickly?

- Why do we talk least about what matters most?

- What does my brain need to collaborate?

- Why do values matter?

- How can I better hear what needs to be said?

- How can I better say what needs to be heard?

- What is a living contract?

- How do I introduce a systematic approach to conflict?

> Our 'opponents' are our co-creators, for they have something to give us which we have not. The basis of all cooperative activity is integrated diversity… What people often mean by getting rid of conflict is getting rid of diversity, and it is of the utmost importance that these should not be considered the same. We may wish to abolish conflict, but we can never get rid of diversity. We must face life as it is and understand that diversity is its most essential feature… Fear of difference is dread of life itself. It is possible to conceive conflict as not necessarily a wasteful outbreak of incompatibilities, but a normal process by which socially valuable differences register themselves for the enrichment of all concerned.

> Mary Parker Follett (Cloke and Goldsmith, 2003)

The book is broken down into six chapters. The early chapters are the most theory-heavy chapters. These set the scene and explain what conflict is and why conflict happens. At the end of these first few chapters I've provided 'Key points to take away', which will help you to remember what you've read. As we get further into the book we're going to start looking at, and using, a number of tools and strategies to help you manage conflict and difficult situations. These chapters are slightly longer and you'll notice that there aren't any key summaries at the end of the chapters. This is deliberate as all the tools are equally useful and will provide a systematic guide to conflict resolution.

Chapter 1: we're going to take a deeper look at what conflict is and why it can actually be the magic ingredient in your life and your business.

Chapter 2: I'm going to challenge you to look at the cost of ignoring conflict or handling it badly, as well as thinking about some of the common issues that cause it in the first place.

Chapter 3: what goes wrong and why? Why do we choose not to disclose things that are upsetting us? When we do find the courage to confront other people about our concerns, why don't we act as we would like to?

Chapter 4: getting down to business – what tips and tools can we use if we want to get things right in future? Learn and practise what you need to do and say to get it right next time.

Chapter 5: we look at how to avoid future problems by creating what I call a living contract based on the five Rs of relational agreement.

Chapter 6: create a systematic approach to conflict. This will encourage you to have a plan in place for managing the inevitable conflicts as and when they arise.

As with other titles in the *Authority Guides* series, this book uses exercises, models and case studies. In the case studies and personal stories you'll read about the way in which other people have put this training into practice in their lives and businesses and you'll learn how to use these examples.

When you've finished the book, if you'd like access to more resources and podcasts, or if you'd like to contact me, you can do so via my website: janegunn.co.uk

The dangers of life are infinite and among them is safety.

Goethe

1. What is conflict?

Do you ever feel that you could do your job more effectively, grow your business more successfully or enjoy your life more if only people didn't get in the way? Or perhaps you've wondered why dealing with other people is not as simple as you would like it to be?

In the workplace, you may feel that you are constantly firefighting and struggling to deal with people who see things differently from you.

All the relationships that we're involved in, whether at work or at home, are bound to run into conflict from time to time. Although this is frustrating and can be a drag on your time and energy, conflict can be a good thing because it provides us with an opportunity to review the way things are and make changes for the better.

A shoe factory sends two marketing executives to a region of Africa to study the prospects for expanding business. One sends back a telegram saying:

SITUATION HOPELESS STOP NO ONE WEARS SHOES.

The other writes back triumphantly:

GLORIOUS BUSINESS OPPORTUNITY THEY HAVE NO SHOES.

> Before you go any further in the book, list some issues that are currently affecting you and that you wish could be easily resolved.
>
> 'Work/life would be easier if _____.'

If you're going to build an effective business culture, or create a happy and fulfilling relationship, you need to be able to do three things:

- Acknowledge and actively manage conflict
- Understand why conflict can be a magic ingredient that helps keep your business and relationships on track
- Use the skills and mindset of collaboration

What is collaboration?

Collaboration is about getting people to work together towards a specific goal or aim. In organisations, whether large or small, people are increasingly discovering the need to collaborate more effectively – both internally that is within and between departments, and externally with their stakeholders. In other groups too, perhaps a family, club or social organisation, there is a need to work collaboratively and to be less competitive and adversarial in our approach when it comes to solving the inevitable problems and challenges.

We live and work in a world of increasing interconnectedness and rapid change, and because of this there is a growing need to improve the way people work together. Getting collaboration right promises tremendous benefits, but despite the number of initiatives and millions of pounds spent on trying to improve collaboration, very few organisations are happy with the results. There are several reasons for this but the primary one is that breakdowns in collaboration and teamwork almost always result from fundamental differences – in other words, from conflict. When this happens, what people need most is not a strategic goal or corporate vision or training in teamwork. What they need is a fast and cost-effective way to identify and resolve the inevitable conflicts without demonising or blaming others and before any of the dysfunctional behaviours that people instinctively resort to start to manifest.

This is why we need to both acknowledge and actively manage conflict *and* to see it as the magic ingredient in our efforts to work things out together.

What is conflict?

Take a look at this checklist of some of the warning signs of conflict. Do you recognise any of them?

- Angry comments or behaviour
- Avoiding meeting or talking to a person
- Being sidelined from meetings or events
- Gossip or conversations behind someone else's back
- Slow work or deliberate delay
- Withholding knowledge
- Sending secret notes or emails
- Aggressive competition
- Low morale, and loss of energy and motivation

These behaviours are the early stages of conflict. We often deny they exist or avoid them because we mistakenly associate conflict with failure and also partly because we lack the knowledge of how to deal with them: we don't know what to do next.

Does this sound like you?

Write down some words that immediately spring to mind when you think about conflict. Examples could include: disagreement, anger, discomfort, dispute and argument.

Did you write down any positive words, such as hope or opportunity? Later in this chapter we'll see why I think that conflict can be positive. In the Introduction, you'll remember that I've used the phrase that conflict can be magic – we'll return to this shortly.

But for now, our definition of conflict is quite simply the process by which people express their unhappiness with another person, group of people or situation.

When we're in a conflict situation and feeling unhappy or angry, most people respond in one of several ways. The most common behaviours are:

- Silence – not speaking to another person
- Talking about them behind their back – gossip, innuendo and character assassination
- Withholding information, so that they fail at what they're trying to do
- Sabotaging their plans or their work
- Fighting – either verbal, or more rarely, physical attacks

When we start acting like this, or see others behaving like this, we often deny or ignore these behaviours because we don't appreciate the danger of doing nothing and we don't have a plan for what to do next. To put it simply, by ignoring conflict and its subsequent behaviours, we allow situations to get out of hand.

Exercise

- Are you angry or unhappy with someone at work or at home?
- Is someone angry or unhappy with you?
- How do you know? What are the signs?

Take a few moments to think about the key relationships in your work and in your home life. Make two separate lists: one for work and one for home. Make a note in the column next to the person's name of any unresolved issues, concerns or unhappiness that you have with that person. In the next column briefly describe the issue or concern and in the final column say whether you think the other person is aware or unaware of the situation.

Name	Issues	Description	Aware?

Most of us will have some issues or concerns in all of our relationships from time to time.

The next question you need to answer is, 'How important is resolving these issues to the continuation and ongoing health of your business, family or life?' And 'What is the potential impact if the matter remains unresolved and how much time and energy are you spending, thinking, worrying and talking about it?' Finally, consider the extent to which it may affect your day-to-day happiness.

Name	Impact	Time/ energy	Happiness

Why do we hate to deal with conflict?

Have you or someone around you started behaving differently? Did you simply ignore the situation and hope everything would soon get back to normal?

Most of us hate the idea of conflict and so one of our most common reactions to it is to fail to acknowledge it, pretend it isn't happening and quite simply to ignore it and hope that it will go away. Sometimes this process can continue for months or even years.

Many times in the workplace, or at home, we are under pressure to get things done, so we don't have the conversations that we should. I recently spoke to someone who had experienced a conflict with a colleague at work that had impacted on both of their lives for over five years. How did this happen? The answer is that both of these people were unable to deal with the situation because they were afraid of what might happen if they had an open and honest discussion about what was frustrating them. Also, they most likely lacked the skills and tools to have that conversation.

Mount St Helens volcano

When Mount St Helens, a volcano in Portland, Oregon, USA, erupted at 8.23 am on Sunday 18 May 1980, people were unprepared and shocked at the devastation that followed. However:

- The eruption occurred *two months* after the mountain first started venting
- There had been *many warning signs* that a devastating blast would happen

Despite these warning signs, 57 men, women and children were killed. Despite predictions of landslides and floods, people were sitting in deckchairs on the bridges to get a better view of the volcano – the watery wall of mud and trees that followed wiped out all the bridges!

Al Siebert, a former Portland resident who happened to be a psychologist and studied what it takes for individuals and organisations to survive potentially disastrous events, suggests in his book *The Survivor Personality* (1994) that there are many important lessons to be learnt from natural disasters:

- We deny danger or potential disruption if it's inconvenient
- Disbelief prevails over reality – even when there are warning signs, most people will dismiss a threat if it has never happened before
- Even when we know that problems might occur, we seldom make plans for dealing with them until they do

When we ignore conflict things begin to escalate out of control. This is when problems become much harder and more costly to resolve.

If you want to operate effectively in business or create happy and fulfilling relationships, then you need to be aware that conflict *will* happen and to:

- Expect it
- Acknowledge it
- Plan for it

Why is conflict like magic?

Earlier in this chapter and in the Introduction I stated that conflict can be magic. Because difficult conversations and the behaviours associated with conflict can be distressing, it may seem odd that I'm associating such a positive word as 'magic' with conflict.

But think about the word 'magic'. Perhaps you think of someone conjuring a rabbit out of a hat, or a stage magician cutting a person in half. Magic is usually where something unexpected happens that goes against natural forces. So if our expectation is that conflict is often painful and usually leads to an unhappy outcome, how would we feel if the opposite was true? We need to see conflict as a catalyst that helps us become aware that something isn't right and search for ways to make it better.

Conflict is like water

Imagine you have a garden that you have filled with beautiful plants and trees. If we have a dry summer and you fail to water your garden, most of the plants will wither and die. However, if we have a thunderstorm and a month's worth of rain falls in just one day, your garden may be flooded and still ruined. Just as your garden needs some water to thrive and grow, so we need some conflict in our organisations and relationships to help them to thrive and grow. No conflict at all is just as bad as too much conflict. So what we need is a way to capture and manage both rainwater and conflict to make sure that our gardens and our organisations and relationships are able to grow and flourish.

Key points to take away

- Conflict is the processes or behaviours by which you or other people express their unhappiness.

- Conflict is to be expected, so you need to acknowledge it and plan for it.

- Conflict can be a magic ingredient as it allows you to open a window of opportunity to change things for the better.

If we keep following the idea of an eye for an eye and a tooth for a tooth, we will end up with an eyeless toothless world.

Gandhi

2. The cause of conflict and why we shouldn't ignore it

The cost of ignoring conflict

Catching conflict before it becomes destructive as well as seeking creative ways to resolve problems and keep relationships on track is the key to adding value instead of generating waste or loss.

Unmanaged or badly managed conflict can have an enormous cost to your business and to individuals and society. It is not always possible to quantify the loss in financial terms but the cost to British business has been estimated to run into billions of pounds every year. A report from 2006 estimated that it affects UK business by £33 billion per year, taking up 20 per cent of leadership time and potentially losing up to 370 million working days. (CEDR, 2006)

The cost to individuals and families cannot be estimated.

What are some common issues that cause conflict?

In Chapter 1 we looked at how conflict can actually be a magic ingredient in your business or life. This is because as long as it's tackled early you have a window of opportunity to turn things around. In this chapter I'm going to go a bit deeper and explore the root cause of conflict.

We've looked at some of the signs and symptoms – what you might see, feel or experience – but where does it come from?

Think of a conflict in which you've been involved. It can be business related or from your personal life. Some examples might include:

- Your business partner is not pulling their weight
- Your co-director is not a good team leader
- Your employees are unhappy with working conditions
- Your partner is late home – again
- Your neighbours are noisy
- Your teenager won't tidy his bedroom
- Your doctor has misdiagnosed a medical condition

Why do these behaviours cause us distress? Why do we care?

Each situation robs us of an element of control.

Any situation that robs us of our freedom by restricting our ability to be independent and make choices harms our self-esteem – the way we feel about ourselves. It's the loss of independence that sparks all conflicts – and is also the key to resolving them.

If someone cuts you up at the traffic lights or your boss criticises a report that you have stayed late to finish – how much power do you have in this situation?

You feel angry or upset because of your loss of power and control. The response to this is to react negatively.

If you already have low self-esteem, then by definition you already feel that you are not in control – then you will get even angrier. In contrast, the higher your self-esteem the less angry you will become in a negative situation.

How you behave depends on how you feel about yourself and the degree of control you feel you already have in your professional life and relationships.

So let me ask you:

How do you feel about yourself?

Our sense of self, or how we feel about ourselves, determines whether we interpret a disagreement with a colleague as a deliberate attempt to undermine us or as a misunderstanding to be resolved.

Every one of us fits on a scale – from being *approval driven* at one end through to *self-actualised* at the other. If we are approval driven we have a high need for recognition and are driven by the approval of others. If we are self-actualised we both realise and appreciate our potential and abilities.

```
|————————————————————————————————————|
Approval driven                      Self-actualised
```

Approval driven	*Self-actualised*
High need for recognition	Authority from within
Driven to succeed;	Open and authentic;
low self-image	high self-image
Need for social acceptance	Self-reliant

Where we fall on this scale will depend on a number of factors such as the impact of relationships with our parents, siblings, teachers, mentors, coaches and so on. Some days your self-esteem will be higher than on others.

Exercise

Answer the following questions as honestly as you can. They may help to give you a sense of your own self-esteem:

- Do you fear being rejected by others?
- Do you take things personally when criticised?
- Do you worry about what others think of you?
- Do you make excuses if things go wrong?
- Do you accept yourself the way you are?
- Do you find it easy to express your thoughts and opinions?
- Do you believe you can handle anything?
- Do you feel comfortable with change?

If you tend to be more on the approval-driven end of the scale, you are much more likely to fear rejection, to take things personally and to worry about what others think of you. You may also be inclined to make excuses if things go wrong rather than accept the blame and apologise.

Does this sound like you? Are you like this – all the time? On a bad day? Occasionally?

What is the cost of unresolved conflict?

When talking about the cost of unresolved conflict, you need to think about how this affects your business or the impact that it has on your home life. At the beginning of this chapter I mentioned a report that revealed some eye-opening statistics. It was carried out in 2006 by BDO LLP (formerly BDO Stoy Hayward) so any financial costs will be dated, but what it did reveal was the level of impact that conflicts had on a business. The most damaging effect of conflict on organisations was on management time:

- 87 per cent of businesses experienced a detrimental impact on management time
- 70 per cent of businesses suffered financial loss
- 89 per cent of conflicts lasted over three years – resulting in high levels of stress and decreased motivation

Exercise

How much might the inability to identify and resolve conflict quickly be costing your business? Add it up!

In Chapter 1, I asked you to think about the key relationships in your work and in your home life and consider any unresolved issues, concerns and unhappiness (page 5).

Take the most serious conflict or dispute from your list and work out the cost of professional assistance, lost revenue from work and personal impact. You may find it useful to use the table at the end of this exercise.

- Have you sought any professional or other advice as a result of this matter? This may be from a lawyer, accountant, counsellor, psychotherapist or any other person treating or advising you as a result of the current situation.

- How much time have you spent thinking or worrying about this issue, travelling to, from and in appointments with professionals, in meetings with colleagues and so on?

- How else might you have spent that time? In particular, in business terms think of the potential cost of lost productivity and missed opportunity. How much more effective and efficient might you have been if you were able to focus *all* of your energy on your work instead of being distracted?

- Have important relationships been lost or damaged as a result of this matter remaining unresolved?

- What impact might this issue have had on your health either in the short or the long term? Have you been experiencing symptoms such as anxiety, depression, insomnia, high blood pressure and so on?

For some of these items it will be easy to attribute a cost or to work out the value. For example, professional fees, medical costs and travel expenses. For others you will have to estimate. For example, how much profit or value might you have added for yourself or your employer in the time you have spent on this?

For the remainder of the items, for example, relationships and health, the cost may be calculated in terms of time off work or the loss of a client and therefore a valuable contract. However, on another level the cost is truly incalculable but I would ask you for the purposes of this exercise to give it a value anyway and one that reflects the value to you of health and relationships.

Be aware that even though you may be working out the cost of a workplace conflict, it will also have an impact and therefore a cost in terms of your home life and vice versa.

Advice	The cost of any professional or other advice you have sought	
Productivity	Time spent dealing with this and productivity lost as a result	
Relationships	Important relationships damaged as a result	
Health	Possible impact on health – short and long term	

The impact of conflict on stakeholders

In the last section we looked at how much conflict might be costing your business or affecting your personal life. But who else should you be aware of when thinking about the impact of conflict?

Whether you're running a business or are part of a family, we all have stakeholders. Stakeholders are interested parties – other people or organisations to whom we are accountable or who are in some way interested in or impacted by our actions or decisions. These people are most often not part of our conflict but they are most definitely affected by it in some way.

Imagine you have a conflict at work and go home stressed each evening and are grumpy with your partner or shout at your children. What if a conflict between your organisation and another threatens to undermine your profitability or might even force you to close down – how many people are potentially impacted?

There are almost always people in the background of a dispute who may influence or be interested in the way it plays out.

Drawing up a stakeholder list or creating a stakeholder chart can help you to understand this.

Let's take a small business as an example – who are its stakeholders?

- Directors/partners
- Employees
- Suppliers
- Customers/clients/patients
- Investors
- Family

- Local community/general public
- Others

Not keeping stakeholders informed

Peter and Rachel were travelling to Hawaii to be married. Their beach wedding would be attended by close family and friends and they were all travelling out together with a well-known airline. When they arrived at the airport the conveyor belt at the check-in desk was not working but their bags were duly labelled and they and their guests boarded the plane. As the plane was cruising the pilot announced that in fact none of the passengers' suitcases had made it onto the plane due to an IT glitch at the airport. As soon as Peter and Rachel arrived at their destination, they tried to find some-one from the airline to tell them when their missing luggage would be arriving. No one could be found and so they set off for their hotel without any of the clothes and items that they had packed for their special day. After several hours trying to get through on the phone Peter posted an angry tweet naming the airline and venting his anger at being ignored.

This is exactly what happens when people feel they are not being listened to or taken seriously. Immediately the conflict has escalated, involving several more customers and potential customers who may have read Peter's message. If it turns out that the IT glitch was actually caused by human error or that the airline were not open and honest in their communications about the issue, then more people become involved. Ultimately this could affect the reputation of the airline and even the sharehold-ers if the price of their shares is affected.

Key points to take away

- Any situation that takes away your power forces you to react negatively.

- How you behave depends on how you feel about yourself and the degree of control you feel you already have in your life and relationships.

- Unmanaged or badly managed conflict can have an enormous cost to us as individuals, a business and a society.

- As well as financial loss, unresolved conflict will lead to decreased motivation and stress.

- Knowing who may be a party to, interested in or impacted by conflict can help you plan solutions.

3. What goes wrong, why and how to talk about it

Conflict often arises when our expectations about a situation, event or someone else's behaviour are not met.

Instead of being aligned or in harmony with the other person, there will be a variety of outcomes, including:

- Differing expectations
- Competing goals
- Conflicting interests
- Confusing communications
- Unsatisfactory relationships

So why don't we act earlier?

The problem is that good and bad points in a relationship are hidden behind a mask or veneer of sociability. Creating a safe way to address issues and concerns is the key to constructive resolution and deeper relationships.

We're now going to look at why it is that we don't deal with situations earlier by saying what's on our mind.

Think about these questions in a conflict situation:

- How do you *show* that you are unhappy with someone or something? How do they *show* you?
- When is it appropriate to say what you think and feel?

The problem with being totally honest and open is you risk upsetting someone. It is the fear of the other person's reaction that prevents us from sharing what we really think and feel. Because of this we don't know when it would be appropriate to take the risk of sharing our thoughts and feelings. And more importantly, we do not know how to say what we want to without upsetting the other person or damaging our relationship with them. Instead of saying something to the person with whom we are upset, we keep our thoughts and feelings to ourselves or share them with someone else.

We also may make assumptions. We imagine the worst and judge the other person. The problem is that because they are not part of the conversation they do not have an opportunity to challenge or correct us. This is what we call 'parallel conversations'.

Parallel conversations

Parallel conversations occur because there is often an exchange of information without one speaker really listening to the other. Because we don't ask questions of the speaker, we interpret what they've said. We end up with the conversation edited by our own perspective, biases, assumptions, judgements and inferences.

Imagine that you have a conversation with a colleague. You're planning a team lunch, but your first colleague suggests that you exclude another colleague from the lunch because she's leaving the business. You feel outraged but you don't say anything.

Here's the conversation, and how it can be interpreted through parallel conversations:

The conversation	My thoughts, feelings and observations
'I think it would be much better if we didn't invite Juliet to join us for the team lunch as she's leaving anyway.'	He's just thinking about himself. I saw him look away when he said that. He doesn't like her.

When we don't address a comment or situation directly with the speaker we tend to infer or believe the worst. We then tell this worst-case story to ourselves and others: we gossip. Rumour takes hold and this is how conflict escalates.

Exercise

Do you know what the people who matter most to you, in business or at home, really think of you? In your everyday conversations, how easy or difficult do you find it to talk about things that are important? On what level do you relate to key individuals in your life?

- Cliché level – you normally engage in 'small talk' about the weather or other safe topics

- Reporting facts – you tend to discuss news items and other facts/information

- Sharing opinions – you find it easy to share ideas and beliefs about life and/or the current situation

- Sharing feelings – you are able to share your feelings when appropriate

- Total honesty and openness

On the chart below enter the initials of your ten names (five business and five personal) at the level at which you feel you communicate with those people. Now you can see how easy you find it to discuss the things that really matter.

Figure 1 Relationship levels to key individuals in your life

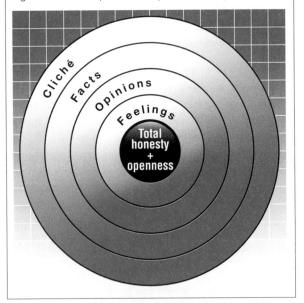

How to find out what expectations are, or how to express unhappiness and disappointment

Imagine that you're at the beginning of a conflict situation. Either you or someone else is using their own biases, assumptions and judgements. You sense that all is not well. What do you do? How do you find out if what you were *expecting* of others has not happened or been said, or discover what the other person or people are *expecting* of you?

Whenever you can, check with the others involved what it is that they were expecting to happen or to be said and why they are behaving as they are. If you need to clarify the situation, write down some key points. Focus on what you were expecting, but also what you think they were expecting:

- I was expecting: _____
- They may have been expecting: _____

When you come to discuss a possible conflict situation, you might use phrases such as:

- 'I noticed that we have not spoken for a while.'
- 'I'm thinking that perhaps you are unhappy about something I have said or done.'
- 'I think it would be helpful to hear what that is because I do not want our relationship to be damaged in any way.'
- 'What do you think?'

Why do you and I see things differently?

Why it is that you and I can see exactly the same situation in totally different ways?

Imagine that you live on your own personal island. You are totally familiar with your own territory – with each twist and turn of the road, with each mountain and valley, with every plant and tree. Occasionally the landscape may change a little as you experience something new. Something that changes your attitude or perception, but on the whole you are happy with the way the world looks. To you it is paradise! We all try to make sense of the external world with reference to our own metaphorical island. It's natural to do this because it creates our foundation or roots, it forms the basis of our personal identity and gives us a deep sense of security. It defines who we are and we feel at home there. We imagine that everyone must live on an island similar to, if not the same as, ours and having established our island we interpret everything that we see, hear or experience according to our pre-existing view of the world.

Adidas Wellness Clinic – corporate pacemaker

An example I gave in my last book, *How to Beat Bedlam in the Boardroom and Boredom in the Bedroom*, is of a visit I made to the Adidas Wellness Clinic in Stockport. My business card had the title 'Corporate Peacemaker' on it but in the context of cardiovascular fitness, the security guard misread it and wrote my pass out as Jane Gunn 'Corporate Pacemakers'.

It's important to remember that mindsets of all kinds have the same effect as living on an island. Religious values and beliefs, professional specialty and attitudes related to age, gender, sexuality and race frames the picture within which we are already operating. These mindsets tend to filter out the possibility that another person might be right.

We interpret everything we see, hear or experience according to our pre-existing view of the world (our island, if you like) and our instinctive reaction to difference and conflict is to defend our ideas and beliefs. It's natural to want to safeguard your views and to reassert your opinions in the belief that you can persuade, or if necessary, force others to change their mind. Being prepared to learn about, understand and acknowledge each other's perspective is the key to good relationships and to resolving conflict.

Are there any circumstances at present where your beliefs, values, religious views, age or gender might be colouring how you experience a situation?

Exercise

Take a situation where you really don't see eye to eye with another person. First of all write down your interpretation and below that the other person's very different interpretation. Then try to think what it is that is most important to you and what it is that is most important to them. Finally, say why it is that you feel so strongly and why you think it is that they feel so strongly. Of course this exercise works best if you are actually able to ask the other person rather than guessing what their answers may be.

The point of this exercise is that it helps you to begin to see things from the other person's perspective as well as from your own.

For example, you may say, 'The way I see the situation is that X is always staying late at work instead of spending the evenings at home with me.'

And X may say, 'The way I see it is that you are always nagging me to be home early when I am busy.'

My interpretation		
The way I see the situation is _____	What's most important to me is _____	I feel strongly about this because _____
Their interpretation		
The way they see the situation is _____	What's most important to them is _____	They feel strongly about this because _____

Why don't I behave/act as I would like to?

Why is it that in challenging situations or conversations we don't always act or behave as we would like to?

Think of a time when you had to deal with a conflict situation:

- How did you react?
- How do you wish you had reacted?
- What is the difference and why?

Understanding yourself and knowing how you react in situations of conflict can help you to be more in control of your behaviour. It is also helpful to understand how and why others may react and behave as they do.

Once we understand this, we can take time to ask ourselves questions about the situation and use our whole brain to consciously decide what the best response would be.

In the conflict situation, how did you respond when your instinctive reaction came into play? What did you do?

- Did you fight – use physical or verbal aggression?
- Did you flee – storm off or walk away from the situation?
- Did you freeze – react as though nothing had happened?
- Did you appease – try to stop the conflict by offering concessions?

Are there other factors involved that could explain your own or the other person's reaction to the current situation? Examples could include: past experience, a build-up of stress, low blood sugar or lack of sleep.

Emotional barometer

When emotion is high – logic is low.

Can you remember a time when you were very emotional about something – upset or angry? What happened if someone tried to talk you down and get you to be less emotional or to solve the problem for you or perhaps to help you see things in a more logical way? Did it work? Probably not! The reason is that our brain is quite literally hijacked by our emotions.

So just like a weather barometer, when our emotions are high our logic is low and we are unlikely to respond favourably to anyone who tries to get us to see things in a more rational light.

Do you recognise when your emotions are high or when your physical or mental state is causing you to react in a different way from how you would like? What tactics could you develop to manage this?

When we're in a place of threat or conflict, we have to teach ourselves to have the whole brain working. We have to accept that what we first experience is instinctive and not reasoned.

Then we have to ask ourselves three questions:

1. What's really happening here – is this a real emergency?

2. What are some alternative realities to my original perception?

3. Who else matters – what matters to them?

Learn to calm down

Deep in our brains we have and area known as the amygdala. This plays a very important role in detecting fear, making decisions and generating emotional reactions. It's a very basic response. In his book *Emotional Intelligence: Why it can matter more than IQ*, Daniel Goleman calls this instinctive reaction an 'amygdala hijack'. It is important to develop your own strategies to overcome the instinctive amygdala response to conflict and to give yourself more time to think.

One of the things we forget to do when we are in a highly stressful situation is to breath. When we are stressed we tend to take short, rapid breaths, which leave us short of the right balance of oxygen and carbon dioxide. Your brain requires the right amount of oxygen and carbon dioxide for clear thinking. Rapid breathing can make you feel even more agitated and in the long term can contribute to other issues such as digestive problems and even a lowered resistance to infections. The best tip for calming yourself down is to become aware of your breathing and to concentrate on making your breaths calmer and slower. The following steps may help:

1. Tell yourself to stop and slow down.

2. Breath in slowly through your nose.

3. Pause for a second or two.

4. Let the air out S-L-O-W-L-Y (this helps to retain carbon dioxide, your natural tranquilliser).

5. As you exhale relax the tension in your muscles – especially in your shoulders and face.

Practising the calming breath can also have a knock-on calming effect on those around you! This is an immediate solution, but in the long term think of joining a yoga, mindfulness or meditation class.

Why does conflict escalate so quickly?

If it is not recognised, acknowledged and managed at an early stage, conflict quickly escalates and becomes much harder and more costly to resolve.

The Austrian expert on conflict, Friedrich Glasl, has helped us to understand how conflict escalates. His nine-stage model from his book *Confronting Conflict: A first-aid kit for handling conflict* (1999) shows us the levels that conflict goes through as it escalates and turns into a dispute.

Stage 1: hardening

Interests and opinions crystallise into fixed positions. Groups start to form around each party and their position.

Stage 2: debates and confrontation

Discussions turn into debates where positions are inflexible and confrontation is more likely.

Stage 3: actions not words

The parties believe that further talking is useless. They increasingly view each other as competitors and the goal is to lock the other from reaching their goal.

Stage 4: images and coalitions

The conflict is no longer about the key issues but is now about victory or defeat. The focus is on gaining the upper hand and on enlisting the support of others to enhance image and reputation.

Stage 5: loss of face

At this stage the aim of the conflict becomes to make the other person lose credibility or 'face'. They become viewed as 'the enemy' and demonised. Maintaining image in the eyes of others becomes important.

Stage 6: management of threats

The conflict descends into threats and counter-threats and becomes increasingly aggressive. Pressure builds and the parties are under increasing pressure to act radically and rapidly.

Stage 7: limited destructive blows

It is no longer possible to see a solution that includes the other person. The aim becomes to inflict loss or harm, and to protect oneself from harm. Survival and less damage than the other is the goal.

Stage 8: fragmentation of the enemy

At this stage the attacks intensify and are aimed at destroying the other person and their basis of power, but to protect one's own survival.

Stage 9: together into the abyss

Nothing else matters except destroying the enemy at all costs even if it means your destruction as well.

Exercise

Think of a recent conflict and identify where it got to in the escalation process.

Can you remember what was most important to you at the time? Was it resolving the issue? Or was it not appearing to have lost the argument?

Why do we talk least about what matters most?

It's much more important to discover another person's needs, interests, fears and concerns than it is to fight to disprove their position on a particular issue. People need to be supported so that they can face their fears and look at the world and the problem from a different perspective.

Winning is not always about attaining or acquiring what we want, but about discovering what it is that we really need.

It's important to remember that there is a difference between needs and interests:

- Fundamental needs. These, when absent, would cause so much pain that they are not negotiable.

- Interests. Things that produce pleasure or satisfaction but about which we, or another person, can be flexible.

Needs and interests may be driven by:

- Fact. What has actually happened and what people expect to happen next.

- Behaviour. How people have treated each other in the past and how they intend to treat them in the future.

- Beliefs and values. People's beliefs, whether based on religion, ideology or personal values, form the basis for their judgement about what is important, good or bad.

  People often find it difficult to talk about their beliefs and values and often fear that others will be suspicious or intolerant of them.

- Identity. Most important to resolving any kind of dispute is people's sense of self, including their sense of what is vital to them in terms of physical and psychological survival.

As well as considering what may be driving someone's needs and interests, you will also need to think about who else is involved in the conflict. It's important to think about the hidden party. For example, if you have an argument with your manager about timekeeping, both your partner and their spouse may be considered as a party because they have an interest or stake in the outcome. That is they will be affected by it. Such parties may not be directly involved in meetings and negotiations, but they should not be forgotten.

Exercise

Think about a conflict when you haven't been able to find a way out. Try to analyse the situation by reflecting on the different needs, interests, fears and concerns of everyone involved. The simple table below will help you to have a much better picture of the problem and how everyone concerned fits into it. It is much better if you are in a position to ask others what their real needs, interests, fears and concerns are rather than guessing.

Needs	Interests	Fears and concerns
What I need: I cannot walk away from this unless I achieve the following…	What I would like: The following are also important to me…	What worries me most: I am concerned/afraid that…
Party 1		
What they need: They cannot walk away from this unless they achieve the following…	What they would like: The following are also important to them…	What worries them most: They are concerned/afraid that…

Party 2		
What they need: They cannot walk away from this unless they achieve the following…	What they would like: The following are also important to them…	What worries them most: They are concerned/afraid that…

Party 3		
What they need: They cannot walk away from this unless they achieve the following…	What they would like: The following are also important to them…	What worries them most: They are concerned/afraid that…

Key points to take away

- When we don't know if or how to address problems directly, we are likely to have parallel conversations.

- If we share these parallel conversations with people outside the conflict it will cause rumour and gossip. The conflict will begin to escalate out of control.

- We all see situations through our own lens and this filters out the possibility that others might be right.

- We need to take the time to learn how and why we see things differently and understand the needs and interests of others.

- When our emotions are high our responses are more likely to be instinctive rather than reasoned.

4. Tips and tools for getting it right

Our ability to collaborate with others to avoid or resolve conflict is based on how our brain reacts in any given situation. But what is it that drives our social behaviour and our desire to work with others? What are the biological foundations of the way humans relate to each other?

Understanding these things helps to make us more aware of the impact of what we do and say in situations of conflict.

Two themes have emerged from neuroscience:

- Much of the motivation driving social behaviour is based on the need to minimise threat and maximise reward.
- Social needs are treated by the brain in the same way as physical needs such as food and water.

These are basic survival responses and are therefore instinctive, but they have a huge impact on our ability to make logical decisions, solve problems, manage stress, feel motivated and collaborate with others.

For example, someone who feels threatened by a boss who is undermining their credibility is less likely to be able to solve complex problems and more likely to feel stressed and make mistakes.

On the other hand, when a person feels appreciated they are much more likely to be willing to do difficult tasks and/or take risks, think deeply about issues, strive to develop new solutions and perform better overall.

The threat response is much more easily activated than the reward response and so the goal in any interaction should be to minimise the threat response and maximise positive engaged states of mind.

What my brain needs to collaborate

Has it ever happened to you that a conversation or interaction with another person hasn't quite gone as expected? Instead of moving towards a solution, whatever was said or done seems to have pushed you even further apart – even though that is not what was intended. Why is this?

It's all down to how our brain reacts to what someone says or does and how this affects our perception of them.

Every conversation triggers a response – the threat or reward response that motivates you to either move towards that person (for example, feel warmer, friendlier, more likely to want to collaborate with or help them) or to move away from them (for example, feel hurt, angry, misunderstood, more likely to want to sabotage their efforts), leading to conflict.

The four Cs of collaboration

Collaboration is the ability and the motivation to work together with others to achieve a specific outcome.

Clearly the threat or reward response is not an ideal state for collaborating with others. There are four pillars that can trigger a threat response or a reward response and we're going to look at these in a little more detail. Applied incorrectly, you'll elicit a feeling of threat in your colleagues, so we'll also explore the best way to use these in order to avoid conflict, or to help you manage difficult situations. The pillars are:

- Connection
- Consideration
- Control
- Caring

Connection

This is about having a sense of safety with, and connection to, others. It's about the relative importance of feeling equal to or better than. Being left out of an activity or meeting creates the same response in the brain as physical pain.

Negative triggers:

- Giving advice or instructions
- Suggesting someone is less effective at a task
- Offering 'feedback'

Many everyday conversations turn into arguments because of the desire not to be perceived of as less than another. For example, people may defend a position even though it doesn't make sense, rather than avoid the pain of a perceived drop in status. For many people the question, 'Can I offer you some feedback?' generates the same response as hearing footsteps behind you at night.

The simple act of giving advice or instructions to someone can be interpreted as though they are less able – and will be regarded as a threat.

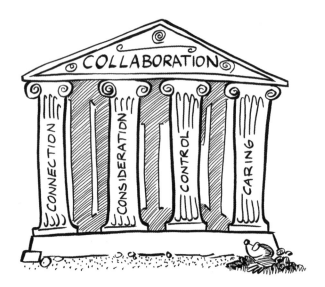

Suppose you've just turned vegetarian or given up sugar – the quickest way to get someone to stop listening and brand you forever as a 'health nut' is to wax lyrical about your new diet, especially if it is the exact opposite to whatever they're doing. Because when you do that, the message you are giving them is that they are wrong and somehow 'less than' you. Even if you don't explicitly criticise or question what they're eating, you're indirectly criticising them. Or at least that's how it might be taken.

A better way:

- Schedule social time together to build trust
- Share more information, not just technical details but also about your thoughts/feelings
- Be open, clear and transparent

Positive feedback and public acknowledgement may help people to feel rewarded.

Consideration

When we feel we're not getting respect from others we get angry. This is because it hurts the way we need to see ourselves and disrupts our ability to feel in control. Anger makes us feel powerful – it gives the illusion that we are in control, free and independent, but the reality is that it makes us lose control.

In every exchange we have with other people we are looking for:

- A sense of fairness
- Respect and courtesy

Negative triggers:

- Perception of unfair dealing or behaviour
- Perception of rudeness or discourtesy
- Perception of giving less time, value and commitment

A better way:

- Better communication skills
- Increased transparency
- Clear expectations

Control

When a person gets angry it is because they are to some extent fearful and this fear comes from a sense of having lost control of some aspect of life: circumstances, understanding of the world or self-image. This could include a sense of control over events or environment or a sense of certainty as to outcomes and the future. Any kind of change generates uncertainty and uncertainty generates a sense of threat. In a workplace environment, micromanaging someone is an approach that generates a threat response.

Negative triggers:

- Uncertainty about the future
- Lack of clarity as to expectations
- Perception of being unable to control events

A better way:

- Making implicit agreements explicit
- Planning together – clear expectations and objectives
- Agreeing boundaries for sole versus joint decision making

Caring

Every person has an invisible antennae, and the moment-to-moment test for trust and respect is, do I matter and am I being heard? If your communication is interpreted as not caring about the other person's needs or of not listening to what they have to say – they will regard it as a threat and react accordingly.

Negative triggers:

- Perception that the other person doesn't care about your needs
- Feeling of not being listened to

A better way:

- Learn to listen
- Care for yourself
- Care for others

Exercise

Think of a recent conversation with someone that didn't go according to plan – for each of the four Cs mark out on the scale below the reaction you felt.

Connection – did you feel more or less connected to the other person? Or did they in some way break that sense of connection by making you feel less adequate or excluded?

Consideration – did you feel respected and treated with courtesy? Or did they in some way make you feel as though you had been treated unfairly?

Control – did you feel that you had adequate control over events and/or the environment and sufficient certainty as to what might happen next? Or did you feel 'done to' and or micromanaged?

Care – did you feel that the other person was genuinely listening to and understanding your needs and concerns and cared about them? Or did you feel that you didn't matter?

Connection	5	4	3	2	1	Lack of connection
Consideration	5	4	3	2	1	Absence of consideration
Control	5	4	3	2	1	Loss of control
Care	5	4	3	2	1	Feeling not cared about

Survival

Al Siebert, author of *The Survivor Personality*, spent his life studying survivors and one thing always puzzled him. In personality terms, individuals have always been assumed as having either one trait or its opposite, for example, being introverted *or* extroverted. Yet, most survivors showed dual personality traits, for example, they were *both* serious and playful, pessimistic and optimistic, self-confident and self-critical, and showed characteristics of both introversion and extroversion. And they could use whichever trait was *appropriate* to the circumstances they were in rather than being bound by *instinct*.

Biphasic personality traits increase survivability by allowing a person to respond in one way or its opposite in any situation. To be biphasic is to be *both one way and another*, rather than one way or another.

Can you imagine how being *both* tough and sensitive, proud and humble, selfish and unselfish, empathic and detached and so on might enable a mediator to work with flexibility and complexity?

Instead of reacting instinctively to a situation or person or automatically according to what you have been taught, biphasic traits make flexibility possible, but being complex is not enough.

The specific pairs of counterbalanced traits a person develops is less important than having *many pairs*. The longer the list of paradoxical or biphasic personality traits that are available to a person, the wider the range of responses available for dealing with a variety of situations.

If having biphasic traits provides options about ways to respond, what determines choices? What gives paradoxical people a sense of direction?

How do they know what to do in unique situations? How do they handle emergencies so well?

How do they know what not to do? Why are they good people to have around?

What has been discovered is that exceptional survivors have a *core motive* and that is the need to have things work well for themselves *and* others.

For example, faced with difficult behaviour from one of the parties to a meeting, you may react instinctively (fight or flight) or according to what you have been taught (toolbox) or by choice (where that choice is motivated by a need for things to work well for everyone).

A person who reacts through choice has been described as having 'high synergy' – beyond what is sometimes referred to as self-actualisation.

High or low synergy?

Ruth Benedict, a cultural anthropologist and author of *Patterns of Culture* and *The Races of Mankind*, is credited as the first person to use the term 'synergy' to explain how humans behave in different cultures and groups.

High synergy exists in an organisation when minimum effort results in cooperative and effective action. Low synergy exists when it takes an excess of effort to motivate people to get things done.

The synergy concept can explain the difference between the effects obtained by managers with a more controlling, autocratic style and the effects obtained by managers where people are allowed more autonomy. For example, low synergy results when a boss sets goals, uses threats, exerts tight control and generally interferes with the way people work. High synergy can be found when a boss enables everyone to participate in goal setting and problem solving and lets people do their jobs as they think best.

People with high synergy are both selfish and unselfish at the same time. They make the world a better place for themselves by making it a better place for others.

Survivors

What can a group of Chilean miners teach us about synergy and how to survive and thrive when times are tough?

On the afternoon of Thursday 5 August 2010 at the 121-year-old copper and gold mine in San Jose, Chile, located in one of the driest and harshest regions on earth, a mineshaft collapsed trapping 33 miners 700 metres below ground.

The buried men became known as LOS 33 – THE 33. At first it was thought that they would not have survived the collapse or that if any of them did they would simply starve to death.

Imagine what it must be like to be trapped underground in the dark and the heat not knowing if you would survive long enough to be rescued.

The miners were trapped beneath the ground for 69 days but they *all survived* and were hauled to the surface one at a time to a triumphant welcome by relatives and the media.

Some of the high-synergy factors that helped keep them alive were:

- Level-headedness and humour of foreman Luis – credited with keeping the miners focused on survival
- Strong vision and belief in ultimate rescue
- Democracy and majority decision making
- Prayer and support from those above ground
- Looking after each other and not just each individual for himself

Exercise

Come up with a list of biphasic or paradoxical traits and think about how they might help you in a difficult or complex situation.

Why do values matter?

When we act or speak consciously rather than instinctively, our behaviour is led by our values – what we think and feel is the right thing to do in the circumstances. Behaviour is a consequence of our values and assumptions – in other words, how we act and react is entirely a result of our thinking. Being clear about what your own values are and why they guide your behaviour can help in managing meetings or difficult conversations because everyone is clear where they stand. Everyone can then be accountable for their behaviours and the values that guide them.

Some useful values to develop that may help you to guide conversations:

- Transparency

- Curiosity
- Compassion

Whatever our values, it is important that they are expressed in a way that is clear and unambiguous.

For example:

- Transparency. I will share all relevant information, including my thoughts, feelings and intentions.
- Curiosity. I am genuinely interested in learning about others' views and concerns.
- Compassion. I will not judge others and will be willing to appreciate others' situations as well as my own.

Values are important because they have underlying assumptions. So if we use the examples above, these are the assumptions that are being made:

- Transparency. I have some information; so do others.
- Curiosity. Each of us sees things others don't.
- Compassion. Other people deserve to be heard. I may be wrong.

If we use these values and have these assumptions then positive behaviours will follow. These are:

- Transparency. I will say what I think and feel and explain my reasoning and intent.
- Curiosity. I will ask genuine questions to learn what others think and feel.
- Compassion. I will show understanding and concern for others.

Exercise

Discover the values that help to guide you.

Think of someone who has really annoyed you. Why was this? For example, they didn't show up to a meeting on time and perhaps reliability is one of your most important values.

Come up with a list of your top five values – the ones that are most important to you in your dealings with other people.

Write them out with a description. For example, reliability means I will do what I have promised to do or give advance warning and a genuine reason if I cannot do so.

What assumption is this based on? Reliability: expectations and time matter and your expectations and time matter to me, too.

What behaviours follow from this? Reliability: I will let you know as soon as I can if something may prevent me from doing what I promised to do and I expect you to do the same.

How can I better hear what needs to be said?

One of the most important skills that you can use to help you to both manage and resolve conflict is the skill of listening. Remember that all communication is about creating understanding.

Communicating

We can express ourselves with great clarity and still fail to communicate. A speaker conveys the message from the perspective of what's important to them. A listener receives the message from the perspective of what's important to them. Unless *both* the speaker and the listener share the same meaning in the message, the words may be totally lost and meaningless.

The key, whether you are a speaker or a listener, is to *show that you understand*. This will give a very clear indication that you are aware of and respectful of the other person's needs, interests, fears and concerns. If you can do this, then the person you are communicating with will begin to have trust in you. They will want to share information with you and join with you in either a conversation or a relationship. If you cannot demonstrate understanding, then the end result may be that the other person will resist your efforts at communication and seek to undermine and avoid conversation and a deeper relationship with you.

Empathy

Every conflict has two components – an emotional component and a rational component. Empathy is the ability to imagine yourself in someone else's position and to understand or intuit what that person is *feeling* – to be able to sense their pain or discomfort and respond to it. The *key thing* to remember is to acknowledge a person's emotional state with an empathic response.

Listening for facts and feelings

> We should all know this: that listening, not talking, is the gifted and great role, and the imaginative role. And the true listener is much more beloved, magnetic than the talker, and he is more effective and learns more and does more good.
>
> Brenda Ueland (1993)

When we are truly listening to another person we are taking in information on two levels:

- We are listening for the *facts*
- We are listening for the *emotions*

Some people are better at listening for and acknowledging facts and some people are better at listening for and acknowledging emotions. However, unless we listen for and acknowledge both facts and emotions, the speaker will have the impression that we are not really listening and don't really care.

These are my rules for good listeners:

- Listen for understanding. What important message is the speaker trying to convey?
- Empathise with speaker. Discern and respond to the mood of the speaker.
- Reflect/playback what you heard. Summarise or paraphrase.
- Feedback your interpretation. Say what you feel and think in response to the speaker's message.

Although these rules may seem common sense, it's important that you develop these skills. Remember that when you're listening, you need to focus intently on the other person.

When you reflect back or playback what you've heard, this should involve 'mirroring' the speaker and whatever they have expressed. You need to capture the full range of what has been said and include a reflection of emotions – how the speaker appears to be feeling. Their silence and reluctance to speak can also be reflected. What is being reflected is any and all communication or expression, not just speech.

Examples of reflective conversations include:

- 'So for you, what's happening is that…'
- 'What you seem to be saying is…'
- 'You're feeling…'

An effective reflection will usually evoke an immediate confirmation:

- 'Yes, that's it', or
- 'That's right and also…'

Even if the reflection missed the mark, it usually elicits a response from the speaker that 'cures' the mistake:

- 'That's not it at all. What I said was…'
- 'I'm not just mad, I said furious.'

Focusing on the other person

True listening is a very courageous act because it involves seriously entertaining the ideas, values and perceptions of the other person and putting your own ideas and instinctive responses on hold while you do so.

Next time you have a disagreement with someone, instead of trying to make them see your point of view, try to adopt an attitude of *total curiosity* and focus all your energy on really trying to understand *why* they believe what they do.

To do this from a place of *curiosity*, 'I wonder what makes him think that way?', rather than one of *superiority*, that is 'I'm right and you're wrong', is the best approach but one that takes a great deal of caring and patience.

Good listening and conversation is at the heart of every successful relationship, and poor listening and conversation is the
root of many relationship breakdowns and the basis of most
conflicts and disputes.

We cannot find personal intimacy without listening. When we
are listening, we are offering the other person the gift of understanding and acceptance (not agreement) – the gift of taking
that person seriously.

Exercise

Think of a recent conversation with another person about
something that was important to them. Now analyse what
the *facts* of the story were. Do you think you were able to
reflect or summarise those back to the person in a way that
made them feel listened to and understood?

Now try to analyse what *feelings* were expressed. This may
be a little more difficult as people often don't say what they
are feeling and we create our own interpretation from their
body language, tone of voice and so on. Did you make any
attempt to acknowledge how the person may be feeling?

Topic What was being discussed?	Facts What were the facts of the story?	Feelings What emotions were being expressed?

How can I better say what needs to be heard?

When we say something, does the person we are speaking to truly hear what we are saying? Do they get the message that we intend them to hear? The message that a person or organisation intends to give is frequently not the message that others receive.

We've spent time looking at how to express ourselves with greater clarity, but even when we do this we sometimes still fail to communicate what it is we want to say. Why is this?

When we are listening – or supposed to be listening – what we actually pay close attention to is the things that directly concern us at that specific moment in time. The same is true when we are speaking.

We believe that people will automatically understand what we are saying and get our message, but unless both the speaker and the listener share the same message, the words may be totally lost and meaningless.

Is their *reaction* to our message what we expected or have we been *misunderstood* or accidently caused *offence*?

On pages 38–43 we looked at the four Cs of collaboration (connection, consideration, control, caring). You should use all of these when you speak to someone. My key rules for speakers are:

- Use 'I' not 'you'
- Share thoughts and feelings
- Say what you need
- Explain reasoning

Try using the following phrases.

To say what you saw/heard and check the meaning:

- 'I think I saw/heard _____. Did I miss something?'

To share thoughts and feelings:

- 'I'm thinking _____. What do you think?'

To explain your reasoning:

- 'The reason I'm saying/asking this is because _____.'

To say what you need:

- 'I need to be able to _____.'

To agree on the way forward:

- 'I think it would be helpful to _____. What do you think?'

Checking in

'Checking in' is when you clarify or check with the other person that you are both on track with the conversation. You are confirming that you have understood each other and where the conversation needs to go next.

'You keep referring to November as a turning point. Would you like to say more about what happened then?'

'It sounds like you might have a lot more to say about _____.'

'We've gone back and forth several times and we seem to be stuck. Would it be helpful to think about other options…?'

All of these suggested sentences could translate into the following exchange:

> I made a request three weeks ago. I don't think I have heard back from you – did I miss something? I'm thinking that maybe you _____. What do you think? The reason I'm asking is because we have a deadline with the client and I'm worried that we may miss that deadline and upset the client. I'd really like to understand what prevented you from responding to my request. I need to speak to the client on Monday and so I think it would be helpful to _____. What do you think?

Exercise

If you have a difficult meeting or conversation coming up, take some time to think about and plan what you might say.

Don't script it out because that won't come across as authentic, but think about everything that you've learnt from this book and how you might use it.

Put yourself in the other person's shoes – how would you react if you received the speech or message that you are intending to give? How else could you say what you need to get across?

What might you do to manage their response if they are upset or angry?

5. How to avoid future problems

What is a living contract?

In this chapter we are going to discuss the idea of a living contract. This is a way of working with another individual or with a team of people where you agree and make clear your expectations and needs at the beginning of your working relationship and agree that you should revisit and update these as circumstances change to keep your agreement 'alive' and manage any disagreement head on at a very early stage.

We enter into contracts and agreements every day. Sometimes these are formal, as in an employment contract or a partnership agreement, but often they are verbal agreements with co-workers, family or friends, making arrangements or agreeing tasks.

Formal or legal contracts are all very well but often they miss out a lot of important details such as *why* we are working together, *what* is expected of us and, critically, *how* we will resolve the inevitable misunderstandings and conflicts that will arise along the way.

All agreements are either express, in other words we are very clear as to what is agreed and why, or implied, in other words we are assuming that everyone knows what will happen and what is expected but it hasn't really been written down anywhere or even agreed on verbally.

Collaboration is established in language by making implicit agreements (what you think the agreement is), explicit agreements (talking to others about what you think the agreement is), and both checking and confirming that everyone has the same understanding.

The idea behind a living contract is that, unlike a formal legal contract that gets pushed to the back of a file and sits there until a problem or crisis arises, the agreement is constantly revisited to check that everyone is happy and going in the same direction, and to catch any conflicts or concerns that might be brewing at the earliest opportunity.

A living contract is based on the concept of interests and needs (see Chapter 3) and on the idea that each party has their own needs and interests that they need to communicate. It is also based on the idea that circumstances will change over time and that therefore the contract should be reviewed and revised on a regular basis.

The five Rs of relational agreements

Reasons

The first step is sharing a *big picture* of what you are doing together as a context for the details. The clearer and more specific the *detail* of desired outcomes, the more likely you will attain them as visualised. You need to think about and agree:

- What do you want to achieve together?
- Why?

Results

The duties, responsibilities and commitments of *everyone* necessary to achieve the desired result must be part of the agreement. For example:

- Who will do what – duties, responsibilities and commitments?
- Deadlines for completion of tasks.
- For what length of time will the agreement be effective?
- What does each of you *need* to be satisfied with the arrangement?
- What evidence is needed that each of you has achieved your objectives?

The length of time the agreement will be effective is also important.

Think back to the four Cs of collaboration. Does the agreement seem 'fair' to everyone involved or is there a sense that one or more parties are giving or getting more than the others?

Review

Circumstances will change and it is critical to anticipate this at the beginning so that the agreement can be revisited. It should be perfectly normal to get together and question whether your original ideas still hold good and whether *everyone* is happy and on track with the agreement. The idea is not to focus on the negative or look to blame anyone, but rather to have a sort of early warning system and to 'take the temperature' from time to time before things reach boiling point.

Collaborative agreements work not because of a lengthy legal contract but because relationships remain intact. For example:

- Think about any change in circumstances and/or your relationship that might cause you to question your commitment to what was originally agreed.
- What will happen for you and others if you do not achieve what you set out to do?

Renew

Change will happen and conflicts and disagreements will arise, so it's important to anticipate this and if necessary renegotiate and renew your agreement. Much in the same way that it is now popular to renew marriage vows, so it should be common practice to renew important contracts to keep them *alive* – hence the term 'living contract'.

Resolution

What we often fail to speak about at the beginning of an important agreement is risks and fears. It's important to anticipate some of the challenges that might arise and to acknowledge that there will be other issues that you cannot yet see. Being open and honest at this time is important. For example, a person I worked with once identified a concern that it was likely that he might make some important decisions without remembering to consult others. This was honest and enabled others to challenge him in the future if it seemed this might be happening. Think about:

- What concerns and fears do you and others have about working together?
- How will disagreements and misunderstandings be resolved?

Is everyone agreed?

It's important at this stage to check and be *explicit* that everyone is agreed on all of the five Rs above. If anyone is not yet clear and/or happy, then you need to go back over the questions until they are. To make sure that the agreement is in the form of a living contract, it's important to think about and agree when and how you will revisit it and how any one of you might raise issues or concerns in the meantime. Sometimes a third party might be appointed to help you with this process. Alternatively, one of the parties to the agreement might agree to take responsibility for checking in with everyone from time to time and calling a meeting to review things as and when necessary.

True collaboration is about working *together* and making mutual decisions as well as being alert for any signs that the working relationship is not on track, and taking early steps to avoid things escalating.

Exercise

Think about people or situations where it would be helpful to have an express and/or written agreement of your expectations of each other – we're not talking about a formal legal contract but something where you can hold each other accountable if things do not work out as planned and that outlines how you will handle any roadblocks along the way.

6. A systematic approach to conflict resolution

When people are faced with conflict and they don't know what to do next, they often spend too much money, too much time and too much emotional energy trying to resolve their problems.

This short chapter introduces the idea behind a system for managing issues or conflicts whereby the individuals involved should be able to choose from a range of options and methods for trying to reach a resolution. They should always start with the simplest and most cost-effective.

Have a plan in place

Having an agreed system or plan for handling conflicts can help us to manage them more easily and at a much earlier stage, and so avoid the problems and costs of escalation.

Know when to act

If we allow a conflict to grow and to fester for too long, it will be much harder to manage and more likely to cause *damage and loss*. If, on the other hand, we can find ways for it to be brought to the surface, acknowledged and dealt with, then we create the potential to *add value* by finding solutions and repairing relationships.

Design a system

A basic design for a conflict management system might look as described below.

Level 1: direct negotiation

The people involved are usually in the best position to attempt to resolve an issue provided that they have:

- Acknowledged the problem
- Have not started the adversarial 'blame game'
- Have the skills
- Are prepared to devote the necessary time to do so

Level 2: assisted negotiation

This involves an independent third party who is not, in any way, involved in the issues between the parties. In an organisational setting this might be a trained mediator or facilitator, but in a family setting it may be a trusted friend, acquaintance or family member.

Level 3: formal resolution

If levels 1 and 2 fail to provide a satisfactory resolution then the issue may (if appropriate) be referred to a higher authority – a tribunal or a court or to a more senior person who can make a decision for those involved.

For this conflict management system to work it's important to agree key details such as:

- The instigator of each step
- How they do it
- By when do things have to happen
- Who needs to be involved
- When it is acceptable to move on to the next step

Remember to include your stakeholders. Ideally, all the people who might use the system should be involved in some way or have some say in its design. The chosen design should present a *preferred path* to resolution, starting at the simplest level with the parties themselves, and giving clear guidelines about when and how to escalate the matter to the next level. If issues are flagged up at an early stage when there is still an opportunity to save and even rescue relationships, then the work of planning ahead and designing a system, however simple, will be worth the time and effort.

General Electric

General Electric (GE) have been pioneers of this systematic or early approach to dispute resolution and believe that they have saved millions of pounds in the process. It began with a commitment by the organisation to use cooperative and not adversarial means to resolve conflicts and disputes arising on a company-wide basis.

1995: Re-examination of the dispute resolution process begins with an analysis of what it costs to resolve disputes on a company-wide basis.

1996–7: The process of institutionalising Alternative Dispute Resolution (ADR): Education (seminars and in-house trainings), Benchmarking (Motorola and Toros), Ad hoc mediations to resolve disputes begins.

1998: The company-wide Early Dispute Resolution (EDR) Programme initiated.

Progress to date

- EDR Programme is a huge success
- Almost all GE businesses participating
- Millions of dollars saved through cost avoidance
- Tremendous satisfaction and buy-in

Concept being expanded

The EDR Programme places GE at the forefront of the ADR/EDR movement – it is possible that they have moved further than any other company so far by:

- Injecting EDR into the corporate culture at GE
- Including EDR as a standard part of managerial training

- Continuing lawyer training
- Weaving EDR into all stakeholder relationships

Creating a culture of collaboration and resolution is a long-term process. Our adversarial system and dispute resolution processes have encouraged a culture of *fear* and *power* that has influenced every stage of commercial relationships, from the drafting of the initial contract to the formalisation of a business relationship, through to the identification and management of ongoing conflicts and the resolution of disputes.

With the growth and recognition of conflict management systems or early dispute resolution (EDR), there now exists an opportunity to change the course of history: to start every commercial relationship with a framework for collaboration, which acknowledges the fundamental principles of agreement.

In a culture of collaboration, the relationship is as important as the contract, and differences and issues can be viewed as opportunities to renegotiate the relationship with optimism instead of fear.

All you need is a plan, a road map, and the courage to press on to your destination.

Earl Nightingale

Conclusion

Books often inspire us and training frequently motivates us to change the way we do things or think about things, but statistics and personal experience show that changing is not that easy.

Three things are needed to achieve positive, lasting change:

- Belief
- Commitment
- Practice

You must *believe* that the change is worthwhile and can bring benefits for you and others.

You must *commit* to doing what it takes to turn that belief into a reality.

You must *practise, practise, practise*.

If you can share your belief and commitment with another person or persons – a friend, colleague, mentor, coach or mastermind group – and take personal responsibility for following through with the required exercises and practice, it will significantly increase your chances of success.

As with any new skill, whether it be riding a bicycle, learning to sing, practising skydiving, when you first begin to practise it's such *hard work* and there's *so much to remember*. But the traits that lead to mastery are persistence, collaboration, and concentrated and reflective practice.

In other words, you must share your belief and commitment, then persist with the task and reflect on your learning. And then you must do it all again and again!

Having at least one supporter but preferably a network of supporters is going to make it all so much easier and more fun.

Will you join the revolution?

I *believe* that now is the moment to start a *revolution* to bring about a movement that encourages people to collaborate, rather than fight, in the face of difficulties and disagreements. This approach can be applied in our businesses, in our families, in our schools, in health care, in politics – the possibilities for change are endless. If each person reading this book can pass it on to another, and so on, we could truly *transform* the way that we relate to and do business with one another on a daily basis.

Revolutions fundamentally change the way we see, think, feel and behave... and thus provide the opportunity for each of us to live a happier, healthier, and more meaningful and productive life.

Expanding consciousness in people – and their organisations – is the only way that we will wake up and stop war, violence, hatred, poverty, hunger, disease, hopelessness, helplessness and the destruction of the earth itself.

There are three simple steps to this revolution. We need to:

• Listen. To learn the skills and to be open to hear and respond to the message that others are trying to get across to us.

- Learn. To be willing to learn from others even when we fundamentally disagree with them.
- Love. We must be prepared to show love and respect to all, no matter what their beliefs, race, creed or colour.

Simple but not easy!

To quote American lawyer Gerry Spence who wrote *How to Argue and Win Every Time* (1996):

> In essence, we remain pre-historic in our approach to conflict. In emotional terms we have not developed as fast as the world around us – this in itself is conflict.
>
> We must learn simple but effective ways to communicate with one another. How to speak, how to listen. How to communicate honestly to achieve our needs and realise our dreams rather than splattering human bodies across the landscape whether metaphorically or in reality.

Will you join me in this urgent task?

If you'd like access to more resources and podcasts, or if you'd like to contact me, you can do so via my website: janegunn.co.uk

You can download free resources including *exclusive* access to an introductory module of my new video series by visiting janegunn.co.uk/download or by scanning this special QR code.

SCAN ME to download free resources from Jane.

We can start a revolution when we know what we stand against. To create change that lasts we need to know what we stand for.

Simon Sinek

Reading list

Benedict, R. (1989) *Patterns of Culture.* Houghton Mifflin.

Benedict, R. and Weltfish, G. (1946) *The Races of Mankind*. Public Affairs Pamphlet No. 85. Public Affairs Committee, Inc. Accessed: https://archive.org/stream/TheRacesOfMankind/pamphlet#page/n0/mode/2up

CEDR. (2006) 'Conflict is costing business £33 billion every year'. 26 May. Accessed: https://www.cedr.com/news/resolutions/Review06.pdf

Constantino, C.A. and Sickles Merchant, C. (1996) *Designing Conflict Management Systems: A guide to creating productive and healthy organisations*. Jossey-Bass.

Cloke, K. and Goldsmith, J. (2003) The Art of Waking People Up: Cultivating awareness and authenticity at work. John Wiley & Sons.

Crum, T.F. (1987) *The Magic of Conflict: Turning a life of work into a work of art*. Touchstone/Simon & Schuster.

Deepak, C. (2005) *Peace is this Way*. Rider Random House.

Elworthy, S. and Rifkind, G. (2006) *Making Terrorism History*. Rider/Random House.

Fisher, R. and Ury, W. (2012) *Getting to Yes: Negotiating an agreement without giving in*. Random House Business.

Fisher, R. and Ertel, D. (1995) *Getting Ready to Negotiate – The getting to yes workbook. A step-by-step guide to preparing for any negotiation*. Penguin.

Fisher, R. and Shapiro, D. (2005) *Beyond Reason: Using emotions as you negotiate*. Random House.

Floyer Ackland, A. (2003) *Perfect People Skills: All you need to get it right first time*. Random House.

Follett, M.P. (2013) *Creative Experience*. Martino Fine Books.

Gerhardt, S. (2004) *Why Love Matters: How affection shapes a baby's brain*. Routledge.

Glasl, F. (1999) *Confronting Conflict: A first-aid kit for handling conflict*. Hawthorn Press.

Goleman, D. (1996) *Emotional Intelligence: Why it can matter more than IQ*. Bloomsbury Publishing.

Lieberman, D.J. (2002) *Make Peace with Anyone: Breakthrough strategies to quickly end any conflict, feud or estrangement*. St Martin's Press.

Manning, J. (2008) *The Finger Book*. Faber & Faber.

Pease, A. and Pease, B. (1998) *Why Men Don't Listen and Women Can't Read Maps*. Orion.

Pink, D.H. (2005) *A Whole New Mind: How to thrive in the new conceptual age*. Cyan Books.

Sacks, J. (2002) *The Dignity of Difference: How to avoid the clash of civilizations*. Continuum.

Siebert, A. (1994) *The Survivor Personality*. Practical Psychology Press.

Spence, G. (1996) *How to Argue and Win Every Time*. Sidgwick & Jackson/Macmillan.

Ueland, B. (1993) *Strength to Your Sword Arm: Selected writings*. Holy Cow! Press.

Ury, W. (2002) *The Third Side: Why we fight and how we can stop*. Penguin.

66

Take time to listen to what is said without words, to obey the law too subtle to be written, to worship the unnameable and to embrace the unformed.

Lao-Tzu

About the author

Jane Gunn FCIArb, FRSA, FPSA is a highly sought-after consultant, facilitator and speaker. She specialises in collaboration, cross-cultural communication and transforming business relationships, and has helped open the eyes, hearts and minds of numerous companies to transform and secure the future of their organisation and the commitment and collaboration of their people.

As a trained mediator and facilitator she brings a diverse mix of skills, experience and insight that enables her to get people and groups, with different priorities, incentives and ways of doing things, to work together successfully. She has a powerful message supported by practical tools and techniques that applies to organisations of all sizes across all sectors.

Jane is chair of the Board of Management of the Chartered Institute of Arbitrators (CIArb) and is a former director and board member of the Civil Mediation Council of England and Wales (CMC). She is a past president of the Professional Speaking Association of the UK and Ireland (PSA UKI). She is also a member of the Advisory Committee to QUADRA in Italy.

She has been invited to speak at the United Nations, the White House, the European Commission and the International Energy

Agency and has fulfilled a number of other international speaking engagements.

She has worked with organisations large and small including Cable & Wireless, the NHS, British Airports Authorities (BAA), Bacardi-Martini, McLaren Racing, The Chartered Institute of Arbitrators, The Royal Institution of Chartered Surveyors, the Association of Chartered Certified Accountants (ACCA) and many more.

She is also the author of a popular book on conflict management, *How to Beat Bedlam in the Boardroom and Boredom in the Bedroom*.

Jane's skill is in getting people:

- Talking about what matters most – both to them and to their organisation.
- Motivated, energised and committed to what needs to happen next.

Her approach is both interactive and fun.

Guiding phrases:

Whatever is unspoken is hardest to change.

We speak least about the things that matter most.

Other Authority Guides

The Authority Guide to Emotional Resilience in Business: Strategies to manage stress and weather storms in the workplace

Robin Hills

How do your challenges inside and outside of work impact upon your emotions and your resilience?

The emotional resilience of those involved in a business will contribute significantly to the organisation's success. This *Authority Guide* from leading emotional intelligence expert, Robin Hills, will help you change the way you think about yourself and the way you approach potentially difficult situations. You will be able to develop your own personal resilience and understand how to develop resilience within the hearts and minds of your team and your organisation.

The Authority Guide to Developing High-performance Teams: How to develop brilliant teams and reap the rich rewards of effective collaboration in the workplace

Andrew Jenkins

Are you making the most of the greatest asset in your business?

To make your good business a great business you need to have more than just a strong product or service. Having a high-performing team in your organisation is guaranteed to give you a competitive advantage. Andrew Jenkins helps you discover how to cultivate in your people the willingness to grow as individuals and as a group. Packed with easy-to-follow activities, exercises and models, this *Authority Guide* explains how to build a high-performing, collaborative, trusting and resilient team.

The Authority Guide to Practical Mindfulness: How to improve your productivity, creativity and focus by slowing down for just 10 minutes a day

Tom Evans

Enhance your wellbeing, creativity and vitality with mindfulness meditation.

In this *Authority Guide*, Tom Evans, invites you to embrace the benefits of meditation in both your life and your business. With the practical mindfulness meditative techniques described in this book, you will learn how to get more done in less time. You will discover how to generate ideas off the top of your head and how to allow serendipity to land at your feet. This book opens the door to a new way to be and do.

The Authority Guide to Meaningful Success:
How to combine purpose, passion and promise to create profit for your business

Tim Johnson

Business results and meaningful work connect to impact effectiveness in our organisations and lives.

Tim Johnson, founder of Meaningful Success, shows you how to integrate practical business thinking with practical personal development to create global impact through your business or charity. This *Authority Guide* blueprints how we can embrace the best elements of entrepreneurial drive and passion, and an enabling blame-free culture to lead high-performing teams whilst providing personal fulfilment for all.

The Authority Guide to Engaging Your People:
Raise staff performance and wellbeing, increase profitability and improve customer satisfaction

Sue Mitchell

Engagement helps business to be more resilient and succeed through periods of change.

This *Authority Guide* addresses how businesses can increase their performance, productivity and customer/staff satisfaction through focusing on engagement. Sue Mitchell, an authority in coaching and leadership development, shows you how to build a team who is committed, inspired and eager to deliver their best work in order to make a difference.

We hope that you've enjoyed reading this *Authority Guide*. Titles in this series are designed to offer highly practical and easily-accessible advice on a range of business, leadership and management issues.

We're always looking for new authors. If you're an expert in your field and are interested in working with us, we'd be delighted to hear from you. Please contact us at commissioning@suerichardson.co.uk and tell us about your idea for an *Authority Guide*.